The model cars
of Gerald Wingrove

The model cars
of Gerald Wingrove

NC

TO
Anthony, Allen, Bryan, Doc and Elaine
for their help and enthusiasm

GRATEFUL THANKS TO

Meccano Limited; the Mettoy Company Limited; The National Motor Museum, Beaulieu, England; Harrah's Automobile Collection, Reno, Nevada, USA; A.C.D. Club Inc; and the many private car owners who have allowed me to use their cars for this work.

Colour Reproduction by
Printing House Reproduction Limited, London.

Phototypeset by
Western Printing Services Ltd, Bristol

Printed in England by Waterlows (Dunstable) Limited
Bound in England by Robert Hartnoll Limited, Bodmin

Photography – Rob Inglis
Additional Material – Gerald Wingrove
Design – John B. Cooper
Editorial supervision and text production – Carole Montague
This book is published under the direction of Allen Levy

New Cavendish Books are distributed by
Eyre Methuen Limited, 11 New Fetter Lane, London EC4P 4EE

ISBN 0 904568 12 1

1906 ROLLS ROYCE SILVER GHOST

Gerald Wingrove belongs to that long line of craftsmen whose work over the years has laid the foundation for this country's reputation in the field of fine workmanship, and I am very proud that I was the first person to commission a model car from him for the National Motor Museum at Beaulieu.

Although Gerald Wingrove is world famous for his miniature automobiles, he is a true Renaissance Man who considers that with application and common sense everything and anything is possible.

This book illustrates many fine examples of Gerald Wingrove's work which should be both a source of delight and inspiration to the modeller and connoisseur of fine craftsmanship.

Montagu of Beaulieu

Contents

GORDON M. BUEHRIG

In the year 1884, Alexandar III of Russia commissioned Peter Carl Fabergé to decorate an egg, to be a gift for his Tsarina.

This work of art and the decorated eggs that were subsequently created by the studio of Fabergé in St Petersburg established the interest and worth of fine art in miniature.

In the year 1951 the New York Museum of Modern Art established that certain automobiles are works of art and they displayed a number of them in an exhibit called "Hollow Rolling Sculpture".

Now Gerald Wingrove has created miniatures of some fine automobiles which, to him, have great aesthetic appeal. He has done this with such skill and dedication that his models may be compared with the priceless decorated eggs of Fabergé.

At least that is my opinion.

Gordon M. Buehrig.

Gordon M. Buehrig

MICHIGAN, USA.

Foreword

Does one *need* to plead the cause of scale model automobiles? Supposing you admire a particular car – the 1914 Grand Prix Mercedes, say, or an A.C. Cobra of the 1960s, to give two contrasting examples. Very few of us can own such desirables, and while photographs or paintings are fine substitutes, only a well-made scale model can recapture the true aesthetics of the beloved machine in three dimensions. And you have the added charm of the *bijou*, the ability to take a reduced edition of the whole in your hands, to view it from all angles, and to appraise the designer's work.

As a one-time professional builder of small-scale model cars, during the bleak 1946–49 post-war period when materials were scarce and plastics hadn't been invented, I came to view the craft as one essentially of compromise and simulation, of 'fiddling' to achieve a car's external characteristics in non-original materials. Striving for 3D accuracy in miniature was a truly stimulating challenge, vastly satisfying when one 'caught' the true character of a subject, but deflating when one didn't. Remembering the better efforts and forgetting the worst, I felt in general that I did a fair job, and carried this illusion along through the years. Then, like the housewife who 'thought her washing was white until she tried Persil', I met Gerald A. Wingrove, and saw what scale modelling really meant. It made my 'washing' as depressingly grey as a modern English spring.

One cannot speak of Wingrove's craft as mere 'modelling' in the lay sense of assembling a plastic kit; it is precision model engineering to the highest degree – the creation of a scaled-down reproduction with total dedication to authenticity regardless of difficulties. It is as much a fine art as painting or sculpture, and I predict that among connoisseurs of *automobilia*, a 'Wingrove' will rate as an essential to all the best future collections.

I called on Mr Wingrove when he was finishing a 1/15th-scale 1930 4½-litre Le Mans 'Blower' Bentley, that stirring machine with its extravagance of lights, stoneguards, filler caps and other complexities so daunting yet appealing to a modeller. To view his model was to look at a real car under a reducing glass. Open its louvered bonnet, poised on exquisite tiny hinges, and there is the big four-cylinder engine in all its detail – plugs, leads, the finned blower manifold, the exhaust system, oil pipes, wiring, armoured cables, oil fillers – the lot. Operate the tiny nearside door handle and the door opens authentically. There were the seats, looking realistically 'used' as if Birkin and his mechanic had just vacated them, the gearbox, the massed instruments, all indisputably accurate

since each dial is a scaled-down photo of the full-sized original. The glorious vee-radiator with is winged 'B', the great finned supercharger thrusting forward underneath, the wheels, hubcaps and tyres – all are superbly *right*.

Yet all this is to 1/15th scale, making a length of about 12 inches (30 cm) – and having 'tooled up' to build one, Wingrove has laid-down materials etc., for up to four more models for subsequent assembly! It is awe-inspiring to contemplate such metallic beauty in 'quantity', the more so when one finds that the Wingrove workshop, self-designed and built behind his home in Flackwell Heath, Buckinghamshire, England, is about the size of a large sun lounge, measuring 13 ft × 10 ft (3.96 m × 3.04 m). It houses a small but highly versatile Encomat 7 centre-lathe, a Mentor milling machine, a power drill, a Paasche 3-in-1 air brush, and a motorised flexible shaft able to take tiny drills, mini-buffs and those frightening high-speed burrs normally used by dentists for much less pleasant purposes. There is also an Emco Star wood-working machine with numerous attachments, kept in an outside compartment between the workshop and the garage, wherein lives Wingrove's Citroën CX 2200.

A dial vernier, micrometer and electronic calculator all play their part in the eternal quest for accuracy, and there are many hand-tools, such as files, pliers, scrapers and delicate tweezers. There is a stock of metals in bar, sheet and rod forms, and a compact Sievert propane welding and silver-soldering torch, all compartmented and cunningly contrived to fold away so that even the lathe hinges inward out of sight, leaving a flat surface for assembly, drawing or other work. Large windows give ample light, the floor is carpeted, a stereo player soothes the occupant with Beethoven or Mozart, and the whole outfit is a masterpiece of 'quart into pint pot' space utilisation, with not a square inch wasted.

The 'Gerald Wingroves' of this world – artists-cum-engineers – are few and far between, and the uncanny authenticity of his work owes much to past practical experience. He spent 16 years with Broom & Wade Ltd, makers of compressors, airtools etc. at nearby High Wycombe, operating centre and capstan lathes and other machines, and modelling ships, aircraft and so on in his spare time. Then he started working from home, making patterns and prototypes for toy companies such as Dinky and Corgi, and modelling futuristic devices for 'Captain Scarlet' of children's science fiction fame for the Century 21 Film Co.

He also produced jigs and prototypes for a Birmingham jewellery firm, and between-times began seeking a specialised class of model engineering. It struck him that few people tackled cars from scratch, chiefly because of the wheel and tyre problem, and one day, flicking through a book on classic cars, he saw a picture of a 1934 Rollston-bodied Model J Duesenberg. That superbly arrogant American extravaganza, with its high, slatted vee-radiator, long bonnet, sweeping wings and commanding overall appearance, captivated him.

He resolved to model it, and sent to the USA for drawings and data, but ironically, an influx of car modelling work for the National Motor Museum and other customers intervened, and his 'Duesey' wasn't finished for several years. As he gained experience, his technique 'jelled'. After working at first to 1/20th scale, he changed to the larger 1/15th, which permits more detail. Not all his models have engines or completely separate chassis, of course; cost forbids it in some cases, while newer model-worthy subjects such as 'Testa Rossa' Ferraris and *monocoque* Grand Prix cars have no such chassis anyway. Wingrove finds that modern subjects afford him less pleasure than older 'classics', which give him 'something to bite on' as he says.

Complication he welcomes as a challenge, and few cars taxed his ingenuity more than the famous 1924 Dubonnet Hispano-Suiza with its open four-seater body and helmet-type wings, all clad in tulip-wood planking, held in place by thousands of tiny brass rivets. Ship-modelling experience paid off here; Wingrove moulded the body and wings in fibreglass, fitting separate doors, bonnet, engine and all the accoutrements, simulated the tulip planking with pear wood veneer, and drilled more than thirteen-thousand '12-thou' (.012 in / 0.304 mm) holes, each meticulously pinpointed to take brass wire inserts, all resined in place and filed and sanded-down flush.

Gerald Wingrove has now built more than 100 car models, and his routine is pretty consistent. Accurate drawings are the first requisite, and whenever possible he seeks out an actual example of the chosen subject and measures it exhaustively. Nothing escapes his steel tape and vernier; he measures *everything* to the last seemingly trivial detail, and fortifies his data with innumerable photographs of the car, taken from every aspect. All available contemporary photos and diagrams are also obtained before he correlates the data and converts it into working drawings. And all this time he will be assimilating the subject, absorbing its aura, and considering its special problems before tackling the job itself.

A 'Wingrove' has the extra merit of being long-lasting. Its maker avoids material which can warp of distort or lift with age, and instead favours metals such as brass, stainless steel, nickel ('German') silver, copper and aluminium, plus fine-grained wood. Parts are joined with minute dowel pins, screws or silver soldering. He is a great advocate of silver, as

against soft solder, both for its strength and a vital extra margin in melting temperatures when making up complex parts. A chassis is fabricated to the correct channel section and taper by laborious machining.

Wheels and tyres being one of the toughest problems in car modelling, Wingrove usually tackles them first. I did the same 30 years ago, and I was pleased to learn that we both employ the same principle in wire wheel construction, turning the rims and hubs in brass, and threading a continuous length of fine wire through tiny drilled holes to form the spokes. But whereas my system was one of compromise, with a machined recess in the hub, the Wingrove way is the proper one, his tiny hubs being accurately drilled with the aid of a dividing head, and the various spoking layouts faithfully reproduced. The result is truly real.

So are tyres, for Wingrove literally moulds them himself. Given full data on any tyre of any age or kind, he can reproduce it with correct tread details plus the maker's name and other wall markings. His secret is a cold-setting silicone rubber as made by Dow Corning of the USA, the Wingrove workshop becoming a mini-laboratory at 'tyre time'. Each tyre is formed in two half-moulds fabricated in hard resin from an original 'master', assiduously made by turning, milling and hand-shaping.

Certainly there is nothing timid about Wingrove's techniques. With accuracy ever the priority, he will vary the method with the job. He will form tricky parts by beating aluminium sheet to shape and soldering them together with a special flux; by spraying molten metal into a rubber mould; or by electro-depositing nickel on to a sensitised glass-fibre former. He made a 30/98 Vauxhall tourer body by beating an aluminium shell around a wooden core, cementing it in place, then machining away the wood to door thickness. And he gold-plates 'period' radiators and other bright parts in preference to brass for non-tarnishing permanence. Above all, this dedicated 44-year old precision engineer is a perfectionist who loves perfection in design. 'I can see it in a car like the Duesenberg', he says, but is never wholly satisfied with his models. 'On each one I make, I see something I could have improved upon. That's why I always look forward to the next one'. Gordon M. Buehrig, famous American stylist and designer of the front-drive Cord 810, has no such doubts. On the fly-leaf of a presentation copy of his book *Rolling Sculpture* he wrote 'To Gerald A. Wingrove, world's best model builder-best wishes. . . .'

(*Reproduced by courtesy of Edita S.A. from 'Automobile Year' No. 26.*)

Cyril Posthumus

Part One

To build models as a hobby you need enthusiasm, to build them as a life's work you need some other factor. I believe that every human being has the seed of at least one added ingredient in his blood, whether it be to play an instrument, excel at a sport, to carve or to paint. The unfortunate thing is that very few have their stars in the right place, at the right time, to be allowed to cultivate their given talent to its fullest extent.

I have been exceedingly lucky, as fate seems to have watched over me in all my work, pointing me in the right direction whenever a fork or roundabout has appeared on the road ahead. My only effort has been to stay with the job in hand and be patient. Now at the age of forty-four, when I look back over the last twenty years (about the time I decided that the only thing I was any good at, and happy doing, was making models), I have the feeling – and it has been very strong at times – that someone somewhere has set before me the right option to take me on one stage further. I have, without exception, taken heed of everything put before me even when I could not see exactly where it was leading, and all these things have led directly to the character and quality that is inherent in my work today. I am as amazed as everyone else that each miniature takes on the appearance of the original when it is completed. Unlike the sculptor who can see his figure in the piece of stone and then carve a foot, a hand and arm, and a head, and find them all in the right place and proportions when he has completed his work, I do not see mine until the final piece is put in place.

For myself I seem to sit back in a trance and watch my hands being worked as if by puppet strings. I still have a fright at the sight of a new project, even though I have now built well over a hundred miniatures, and it is not until I can sit down and relax with all the data spread out in front of me that everything falls into place and the problems fade away.

It is said that some people are born with a silver spoon in their mouth, but I think I must have had a penknife and a piece of wood in my *hand*, for my earliest recollection of childhood is sitting at the kitchen table with my father, watching him build for me a most complicated flying model of a Bristol Blenheim airplane. I think it must have crashed first time out, for I well remember spending many happy hours with the broken off front end, fitting out the cockpit with clocks and controls etc. It would seem that right from the earliest time my bent has been to make something that looks right, rather than something that works.

Having had a very dull schooling, during the war years, fate first seemed to show her hand at the start of my two years' National Service, for the training as an airframe mechanic in the RAF put me in contact with all the metal and wood working tools I use to this day. Not only that, but I was posted to Egypt for eighteen months, and, due to the heat, we were only called upon to work for the first half of each day.

With a nice set of tools, plenty of scrap materials, a few odd paints etc., every afternoon free for a year and a half and most of the places of interest out of bounds because of the Suez trouble, the only thing I could do was make models. Kits were almost unobtainable in the Middle East, so of necessity almost all the work was scratch built. My interest at this time, as could be expected, was in aircraft. However, they were not military, my subjects were Comets, Britannias and the Princess flying boats. This last gave me my first piece of publicity, as 'Model of the Month' in *Aeromodeller* for May 1954.

I also built my first two model cars at this time, one being a kit of a pre-war Maserati about 1/43 scale if memory serves me right, and the other a 50 per cent scratch built post-war Maserati, using wheels etc., from another kit. At this time kits were still basically wood and metal, the car body being supplied as a roughed-out, but squared, block, the modeller being required to round off the corners, complete the shaping and hollow out the interior. The modeller also had to achieve a high gloss paint finish on the outside, and this was my first introduction to the superior qualities of cellulose finishes. (The only ones readily available on an RAF station in the middle of a desert, as they were used on the aircraft.)

After my demob from the services I returned to light engineering as a centre lathe turner. What with drifting through several jobs after leaving school and then compulsory National Service, I missed out on the chance of an actual apprenticeship in engineering. However, this turned out to be an advantage, for whereas the apprentices were moved from department to department throughout the factory every few months, picking up a little knowledge on a lot of subjects and crafts, I spent several years at a time on different machines, which gave me a very thorough understanding of all aspects of machining different metals.

In retrospect, I feel I was also very lucky in the timing of my entry into industrial engineering, as it was just approaching the end of an era. Within about five or six years of my demob the first signs of 'work study methods' were being introduced. Today, under these systems which are now almost universal, a vast army of people are employed to serve the machinist with everything from ready-made tools to the last detail of how he should operate his machine. All the poor machinist is left with is to turn the handles like some robot.

When I started in engineering the practice was for skilled setter operators. This meant that you were expected to be able to make a component on a lathe for instance, on simply being given a drawing. You had to make and grind your own tools and decide the best way of setting them up in the machine. This not only made factory life somewhat more interesting, but it also made for a highly skilled and competent lathe operator. Even so, after the first few years back in the factory I decided that this would not comprise my life's work. Even the administration side did not offer the complete freedom of thought I was beginning to look for. At best it was just a rat race and at worst you had to wait until someone died before you could move up the ladder.

After considerable thought I decided that my real talent lay in making things. It did not matter what they were or from what materials. I seemed to have this feeling for creating something out of virtually nothing. As I did not want to be restricted to work in only one material, as would be the case if I took up silversmithing for instance, I felt the best chance I had of doing something worthwhile for a living (and deriving considerable pleasure at the same time) would be found somewhere in model building, particularly in view of my 'amateur' experience in the Middle East.

I recognized that if I was to call myself a model maker, then I would have to make models of anything and everything, so I gave myself from five to ten years to learn everything I possibly could about the practical side of efficiently working materials to any given shape or finish. This did not mean night schools and theory, but involved spending time with and talking to as many of the older generation of craftsmen that were part of factory life at that time. I joined the local library and read up on every subject from leather work to jewellery making. In the evenings and at weekends when I was not reading I would build finely detailed ship models or put together marquetry pictures, both of which were very good relief exercises for someone engaged in engineering and metal work during the working day. During this time my work area progressed from a kitchen table to a portable tool box, to a tool chest on legs that made up into a work table, to a large work bench in the back of my garage and finally to a ninety square foot workshop which I designed and built onto the back of my garage.

Not long after the workshop was completed (about seventeen years ago), I received my first contact with a professional model maker. The head of a company who was looking for someone to take on part of an order to build a number of super-detail model aircraft for a museum in Canada. After seeing my workshop and my ship modelling he felt I could do the work. However, I was not quite so confident. The project called for some first world war fighter aircraft with built up rib and frame in brass and covered in silk. As I had not at that time attempted such sophisticated models I settled, initially, for building myself an example to see whether I was able to reach the necessary standard.

After several weeks of burning the midnight oil the model was complete. It depicted an S.E.5A. with a wingspan of about twelve inches. My prospective employer was very pleased with the end result (as was I), and the job was again offered to me. However, the terms of employment had changed in the intervening time from working in my own workshop for 90 per cent of the time, and visiting the works perhaps once a week, to spending most of my time at the factory and only doing the odd job in my own workshop. What put me off was the fact that I would have to drive about twenty-five miles each way to get to the factory, so I stayed in light engineering and contented myself that I was at least on the right road with regard to my modelling.

A year later, through a friend, I met a dealer, who bought and sold models. During the course of our conversation I enquired about the modelling fields that held the most promise and learnt that these were armour and cars, both of which were of little interest to me. Up to that time my main preoccupation was with researching details for and building models of some of the more interesting sailing ships of the 1890s. As I had reached the point of perfection in this work, even to making a miniature rope walk to make the scale rigging on, I decided to take my education a stage further and peruse the possibilities of producing a scale suit of armour.

I located several books on the subject and contacted several museums and collections to find out if it would be possible to photograph and measure a set of parts, so that I might put together some working drawings. All the data appeared readily available, I even made contact with a curator in Switzerland who was willing to send all the necessary information on a particularly beautiful set of about 1600.

In view of the lack of problems involved in locating the data and making the basic plates, and as there were enough techniques readily available in the fields of etching and plating to cover most of the decoration, I also decided to have a quick look into the possibilities of car modelling before making a start.

Being a complete novice as regards the innumerable makes and styles that this form of transport has evolved through since its inception, I approached the local branch of a well-known book shop one lunch hour. Thumbing through the usual varied selection that is almost always available I still could not make up my mind as to exactly what I was looking

for. Then I flicked through a small colourful picture book called *The Batsford Colour Book of Classic Cars*, and there it was on page 50, a piece of machinery that struck me as so perfect an example of an automobile that it took my breath away, and it still does to this day. The vehicle was a 1934 SJ Duesenberg a name I had never heard of. However, I was determined from that moment on to find out as much as possible about these cars, with the eventual aim of making them the subject of my entry into auto-modelling.

After much searching I was introduced to the Auburn-Cord-Duesenberg Club in America, the country of origin of the mighty Duesenberg. I joined the Club in 1966 and have been a member ever since and will ever be indebted to its members for the help and assistance they have most generously given me in researching data for this – in my opinion – most beautiful piece of machinery man has ever put on four wheels.

I seem to be wandering a little, I always do when I think of those fabulous cars. However, we will come back to them a little later in the story. Suffice to say that I had found a subject in this field that far surpassed, in personal appeal, anything I had seen in the area of miniature armour. There were, however, two major problems to be overcome. One was how to make rubber tyres and the second, how to produce a spoked wire wheel.

Regarding the first of these, I decided on a double approach. First I obtained from the local library several books on rubber moulding techniques, which gave me enough information to convince me that this was an industrial process and not for the small workshop. However, on receiving several quotations for model tyres from rubber manufacturers, I

The Mercedes Benz truck cab patterns. My introduction to pattern making and professional model making. Patterns for the Meccano Dinky Toys S.P.V. seemed to cover the remaining problems not given to me by the first set, there was hardly a straight line on it. A sample of the pattern and prototype work undertaken for Meccano Limited.

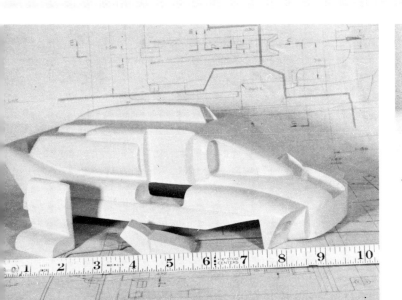

15

was also convinced that this angle was going to be a non-starter. On returning to one of the books I noted a half-dozen-line reference to a synthetic cold curing rubber, which after a great deal of further searching for a supplier, turned out to be the answer to my first problem.

The technique I evolved for making my wire wheels took one week of my annual summer holiday from my engineering job to work out, and once perfected, has served me through all my model cars. It consists of threading short lengths of steel wire from hole to hole around the rim and hub in such a way that any number and patterns of spoking can be reproduced. With these two problems solved, the remainder of the work involved in producing an autominiature appeared to be standard model making.

During all this time I was, of course, still working by day as a machinist in a factory, and had been offered several chances of promotion. I did, in fact, take charge of a machine shop night shift for twelve months, but returned to machining so that I could give all my concentration to perfecting my modelling techniques in the hope of eventually changing trades.

The ball really started rolling when I answered an advertisement for a model maker in the *Model Engineer* magazine in late 1966, the only advertisement I have ever answered, and I would not have written to this one had it not been a box number. Before the week was up I had received a reply from none other than 'Meccano Limited' in Liverpool, some two hundred miles from my back door.

In my letter I had enclosed several photographs of examples of my work, and these evidently made a very favourable impression on the directors of Meccano, for I was invited to visit them at my earliest convenience. I felt I could in no way work for them and travel that distance and, with a wife and two young children, I did not wish to up-house and move either. However, I felt that fate was showing me the way, and that the reply from Meccano was so complimentary that it would at least be an experience for me to go up there for a day and find out what they had in mind.

Taking a day off from my engineering job and starting out at about 5 a.m. one cold and frosty November morning, I drove the two hundred miles to Liverpool, which in itself turned out to be quite an experience. About twenty miles out I hit a patch of black ice and skidded across a roundabout bursting one of my front tyres in the process. However, after changing the wheel I got on my way and was with them in time for my appointment at 11.00 a.m.

On seeing the samples of my work I had brought to show them they still seemed favourably impressed, so they unveiled the work they had in mind for me, which was pattern making for their Dinky diecast toys. This in truth could not be much further from centre lathe turning, the only job till then that I had actually been paid to do. The reason, of course, for using a model maker to make patterns for this type of subject, as against a pattern maker, is in the different approach that each has to the subject. A pattern maker views his subject as an engineering exercise, whereas the model maker will always have the aesthetic view in mind and take only the minimum of licence to fit his subject into a set of tools.

As they seemed confident I could do what they wanted and were agreeable to my doing their work at home with perhaps only visiting them once a month, I said yes and returned home with a set of blueprints and a large block of hardwood.

At this time the only power tools I had were an electric drill and a miniature Unimat SL lathe, but I did have a number of hand tools, chisels, saws, and files etc. After several long weekends and many late nights, I had the patterns complete, even to the limits of plus and minus five thousandths of an inch and plus and minus half a degree on the tapers. Although I had of course worked to these limits in metal with my engineering work during the day, this was the first time I had tackled this with actual hardwood. Today, I machine wood (only of the best quality) in the same way I machine metal.

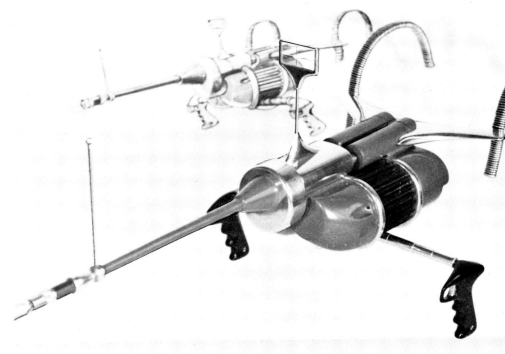

Film Props, from ray guns to old railway engines. Anything and everything can be called for and in most cases it is wanted for yesterday!

After a less eventful second trip to Liverpool, I hesitatingly returned their drawings and presented them with the patterns, which I was relieved to find they were delighted with, and in fact used to produce all the cab parts for the Mercedes Benz LP1920 truck No. 917.

Over the next two years I was to build for them as a freelance working from my own workshop. I made a number of prototypes and patterns, including the originals for the Boeing 737 No. 717; Spitfire Mk II No. 719; Spectrum Pursuit Vehicle No. 104 and Joe's Car No. 102. During the research and work on the latter two models, I was brought into contact with the 'Century 21 Company' who were at that time making some of the most realistic puppet films that have ever been produced, using models and very elaborate miniature film sets. The S.P.V. and Joe's Car, were in fact based on two of the vehicles used in some of their films.

As luck would have it these film studios were only about ten miles from my workshop and a small factory was at that time being built to make the models for use in the films which was only two miles from my home. It was more or less left to me to research each project and design the working parts and, therefore, it was a very small step to leave my factory job as a centre lathe turner and join the staff of the film props division of 'Century 21' as head of toy developments. I had been a turner for sixteen years and it was almost ten years from the time I decided to teach myself model making. I sometimes think they were sixteen wasted years, but then I remember that without that experience, particularly the practical experience of having to find the most efficient way of doing everything, I probably would not be doing the work I am today. I have never considered it a recommendation to spend five years building a single model as some people seem to feel. Speed and efficiency can go hand in hand with quality and detail, when in the hands of a craftsman. In fact, I think they can contribute to the feeling and character of the finished work because the confidence is reflected. How many models, and works of art for that matter, have been spoilt by either being too perfect or by having too much finicky detail, both prerequisites of uncertainty or the artist not knowing when to stop?

So I was now a professional model maker (but unfortunately not a happy one for very long). As only one toy was developed from each film series, which did not take too much of my time I began to drift into designing and building some of the smaller film props themselves, which though very interesting afforded little prospect for the future. My time was not wasted, however, as far as my present work was concerned. The diversity of work I was handling, in a wide variety of finished materials, to a perfect standard and at great speed (as is the nature of the film industry) was just another lesson in improving my efficiency.

By this time I had made a start on building a model Duesenberg (in my spare time, of course) having accumulated sufficient data to draft a set of plans for one of the few right-hand drive chassis produced. The car was to be a model 'SJ' with a speedster body by Gurney Nutting, built in 1936 for a Maharaja.

I had decided on a scale of $\frac{3}{4}$ inches to 1 foot to give me a model about sixteen inches long. I produced a set of six wire wheels, the chassis frames in brass, wooden body patterns and moulds and a fibreglass body.

Starting to get itchy feet again and not knowing exactly which way to go, I began writing to museums and indeed any people I could think of who may require models to be built. Because of my new found interest in cars, one of my first letters was to the Montagu Motor Museum. It was almost as if someone had been leading me in that direction all the time, as they were looking for someone to build model cars.

The original Duesenberg project, wheels, frames, body patterns and engine. My first attempt at car modelling. Unfortunately, they never did get put together.

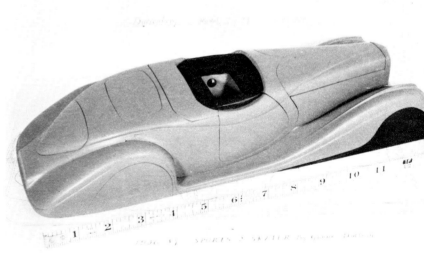

After a very pleasant interview with Lord Montagu, during which my six wheels, one chassis frame and part of a car body played their part, I was commissioned to build two car collections for the Museum. The first was to show the evolution of the sports car from about 1913 to the present day, and the second, to build a model of the World Championship Grand Prix car each year.

With this work, the promise of more from Meccano and some additional work from a Birmingham jewellery company to produce the prototypes for charms, pendants, earrings etc., I felt I was ready to go my own way.

'The Evolution of the Sports Car' – part of the collection commissioned by Lord Montagu, for the National Motor Museum at Beaulieu.

Part Two

In October 1967 I launched myself into the 'unknown' as Gerald A. Wingrove (Model Engineer) builder of miniatures, without any specific terms of reference.

With the Montagu Motor Museum commissions, car miniatures played a prominent part in my work right from the outset, although in the first three or four years it never exceeded 50 per cent, the other half of my work comprising toy development and prototype work, jewellery, and scenic modelling for museums.

To assist me on my way, Meccano very generously kept me well stocked with work for the first few months, but as I had already experienced, the prototype stage of developing a new toy is probably one of the smallest parts of it, the main effort of time and money being the cutting of the steel casting dies. Thus, by early 1968, their work had dropped off to almost nothing. By then I had several model cars to build for the museum collection and I did not seek to renew my contract with Meccano.

Towards the end of 1968, in an idle moment, I again turned my attention to the diecast toy car. All my previous work had been the development of ideas for others, so I sat down for half a day, with the sole aim of creating something myself, something that had not been produced before in the small-scale diecast field. What I came up with was a king-pin steering system for a racing car whereby the driver's body is tilted to one side or the other to turn the front wheels. In fact, I built, or rather modified, two diecast toys and fitted them with this steering, one was a grand prix car and the other a saloon with a small button on the side, in place of a driver to steer it. It so happened that both the toys I had modified had been made by Mettoy Corgi Toys, so I wrote to them offering to sell them back their two diecast miniatures modified for a sum considerably in excess of what I had paid. The outcome of this little enterprise was an invitation to join the Company as a sort of freelance consultant and this I did for the next two years, undertaking though with a much freer hand, similar work to that which I had done for Meccano.

The little steerable racing car was snapped up by Mettoy and later appeared as the Corgi Toys Cooper-Maserati. It gave me a great sense of achievement to see it in the shops, more so than from anything I had done up to that time. Another original I designed for them was the Corgi Comics Lunar Bug. In this I endeavoured to incorporate the maximum amount of play value. The vehicle is in fact as versatile as the child's imagination, as it can be a boat or hovercraft, is suitable for roads or cross country and, if you pull out the folding wings, it can fly – in the imagination at least! If you add to this the fact that it has a fold-down ramp so that the child can also carry other cars in it I felt it covered just about everything.

My pattern making skills were stretched to their fullest with Mettoy when I was given the job of producing the patterns for the Silver Shadow Rolls Royce and the Chevrolet Corvette Sting Ray Coup. Unlike the Mercedes Benz truck cab, these were to be made in metal throughout. Each was between eight and nine inches long and required to be exactly like the final diecast toy, even to the correct functioning of the opening doors and hood etc. Each was also a mass of very close engineering tolerance, not only of dimensions, but also angles and tapers.

It was evident from the start that I was going to need something more accurate and substantial than the tools I had used to make the wooden patterns, so I purchased what has since turned out to be a second right arm – an Emcomat combination lathe and milling machine. Fate had again taken a hand, for this was a unique machine that had only just come onto the market. My local engineering tool suppliers had just taken delivery of their first batch and had one on display in the front of their showrooms, when I visited them shortly after returning from the Mettoy works, with this new pattern work. Within a week I had one fitted up in my workshop and it has been the centre-piece ever since. Had I designed a machine to suit my particular needs, before or since, it would look exactly like the Emcomat, and I now had the work that would make it viable, for this sort of machine was not cheap.

As I completed the second of the patterns (late 1969), I was asked if I could build a model to record the life and times of a small Hampshire village and shipyard in the early eighteen hundreds. Always on the look-out for variety in my work, I

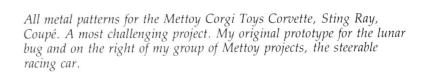

All metal patterns for the Mettoy Corgi Toys Corvette, Sting Ray, Coupé. A most challenging project. My original prototype for the lunar bug and on the right of my group of Mettoy projects, the steerable racing car.

23

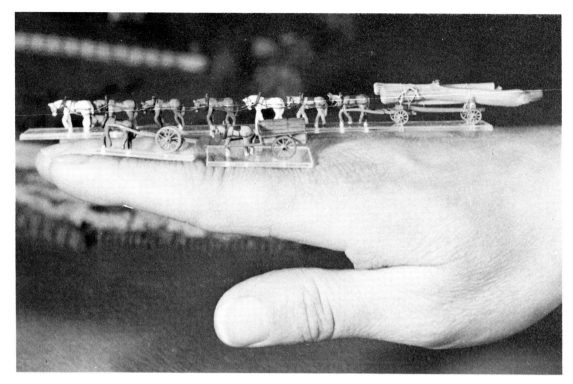

Vehicles with a difference, two of the diverse subjects that have interspersed the car modelling projects. Transport 1803, one-to-two-hundred scale. Items from the twenty-five square foot Bucklers Hard model and a twelve-inch-high model of a combine harvester.

accepted and for the next four to five months I was in my element.

This commission was once again from Lord Montagu and would depict the village of Bucklers Hard, which is on the Beaulieu river, as it was in the days of Nelson, when the ships for his fleets were being built. I was given a completely free hand, with access to all available data and people on the Beaulieu estate who could help. The date chosen, was Friday 3 June, 1803. This enabled me to show a completed hull ready for launching, HMS *Euryalus* (36 guns) was in fact launched on 6 June, 1803, together with a partly built hull. This latter was of HMS *Swiftsure*, a 74 gun man-of-war, which was completed and launched from Bucklers Hard in 1804. As the village was always packed with people and coaches on a launch day, we settled for the last working day before, in order that I could show something more typical of a working day in the village and shipyard.

I chose a scale of one to two hundred, which still enabled me to show people doing their everyday work (in fact there are over sixty people shown working on the model), though not too big to handle on a single base board. The final size being five feet by five feet, the largest model I have so far built.

When completed, it was made the centre-piece of the new Bucklers Hard Maritime Museum. After this major commission I returned to modelling cars for Lord Montagu's other Museum. As it has always been my practice to do my own research for whatever I make, I came more and more into contact with the classic and old sports car enthusiasts who owned and maintained the subjects I was building as models. Inevitably some of these also commissioned miniatures of their cars and incidentally, some have become collectors of my car miniatures in general. For the next few years my work consisted of car miniatures, interposed with museum models of various sorts, from windmills to forts, to a combine harvester and scale models of scientific instruments, some of which can be seen in the Commonwealth Institute in London and the Evoluon Museum in Holland. As my car miniatures attracted more and more publicity, demand from collectors became such that for the past four or five years my work has been almost exclusively devoted to them.

Right from the start I felt that the car, as a modelling subject, would need a completely different approach from almost any other, in particular that of ships and aircraft. Although both of these are made in their original full size form with the aid of tools and machines, man plays a much bigger part in their final shaping and individual character than he does with the automobile. The car, to me, is essentially a machine-made object, relying for its character as a subject on the inherent qualities obtainable from dies, moulds and engineering accuracy. It is so positively precise. The reason for this, I think, is to be found in the wheels, for no other subject that I can think of has so many precisely placed and precisely detailed features as the four, five or six wheels, particularly wire-spoked ones, as the car. This precision is repeated throughout, if one point is not identical to a second, then it is a mirror image of it, as for instance the two halves of the chassis frame, or the left- and right-hand fenders.

With this in mind I decided, when I first looked at the car as a modelling subject, I would make use of as many tools, moulds and dies as possible in the construction of the miniatures. I would then get that feeling of sameness for repeated items that was going to be the key to capturing at least part of the character of the original. As I stated earlier, the very first item I tackled was the rubber tyre, and it was treated in this way, rather than trying to make them individually. One was very painstakingly produced, regardless of time and tooling, to be used as a pattern for making a mould, from which any number of identical copies could be reproduced.

When I set the lathe up with the necessary tools for turning the wheel rims and hub parts, all the pieces are made at the one time so that they can only be identical. It soon became apparent that the time required to make the patterns, moulds, or even set up the machine was often more than that which was actually needed to make the required parts. However, several sets of parts could be made from the same moulds or machine settings with very little extra effort or time. Thus it has been my practice, with the exception of two subjects, that whenever I start a new car miniature, enough parts are made to build up to three or four. I never build more than four at any one time, as I feel I would start to lose interest, and they would become like sausages from a sausage machine. As it is, four cars, each with six wheels, with over seventy spokes in each wheel, usually taxes my enthusiasm and patience to its limit.

I mentioned previously the character of a car as a subject. Although I feel the underlying essence of this is to be found in its precision, the individual character is also to be found in its being, in its completeness and mobility. For instance, the difference in character between a stately old Rolls-Royce town car and last year's world championship Grand Prix car, must in part, at least, be the feeling it gives one, and how it gets from point 'A' to point 'B'. If you read about this aspect of cars it is one thing, but to go and see, smell, hear, ride in or even drive the subject of your model is quite another. So another point I made a note of when I started automodelling was to go and see the subject I was to model, and get the feel of it before my building started. The further advantage of coming face to face with the actual car for an hour or two is that you can collect enough dimensions and photographs to produce a good set of working drawings.

Having found the car, I take up to a hundred-and-fifty black-and-white photographs, together with (in most cases) a dozen colour shots. After these some rough sketches are drawn, to which are added about two hundred dimensions working to the nearest quarter inch. I also keep with me a very useful book of over four hundred coded colour samples to check the paint and upholstery colours. If engine detail is called for in the miniature, then sketches and dimensions as well as photos are also taken of this. Useful as all this data is, it is as nothing without the actual contact with the beast, for it is this that will put life and feeling into the finished article and make it a miniature of the *original* rather than just another model.

It is obvious that there are far more dimensions on a car than the two hundred or so that I make a note of, yet I still have to produce drawings for and construct pieces to represent, almost all of the vehicle. Strange as it may seem, I cannot explain how these pieces come out looking correct, for it is, on the surface at least, only done by guess-work. However, below the surface I think something else is at work, for in practice I invariably spend all my spare time in the two weeks prior to starting a new project, thumbing through the photographs and data. I seem to be able to get into a completely relaxed state, and by some means or other I seem able to absorb the details and proportions of the subject. Once I have gone through this stage I can think of nothing but building the miniature. It is an almost automatic process, once it is set in motion, eating and sleeping, and everything else for that matter, becomes secondary to completing the model. Once started everything I draw or make seems to look correct; in fact, I find it quite frightening at times, for the parts appear to take shape without any particular mental effort from me. Looking back over a hundred or so models I cannot think of any single item, big or small, that has had to be made twice because the first was made wrongly and did not fit or contain part of the character of the final miniature.

All this is not to say that I do not get bored and frustrated from time to time. I must plan my work carefully in order that it grows before me, otherwise my enthusiasm is inclined to evaporate.

I can perhaps best illustrate this, by relating the sequence of events that led to the completion of the 1963 250 GTO Ferrari (page 87). I was particularly enthusiastic about this project for it opened up several new fields. It was the first of many cars that I have now built to the new larger scale of one to fifteen, chosen because it allows room to include the maximum of engine detail, opening doors, working door-catches, etc., without being so big that it looks like a child's toy. (All the Montagu Motor Museum models are built to the smaller scale of one to twenty.) It was also my first saloon and the most modern sports car that I had been commissioned to build. All went well at the start, seeing the car and collecting the necessary data, drafting the plans and checking them against the actual car.

I had noticed right from the start of my serious modelling, that enthusiasm can wane in proportion to the amount of repetitive work that has to be done. For this reason I always

start building a car miniature from the ground up, as it were. First the tyres, then the wheels and spoking. By working in this way the motivation only begins to fade by the time the last of the wire spokes are fitted, which in the case of the Ferrari's was only about twelve hundred, although they were in just about the most complicated patterns. With the wheels complete I then aim to get the axles, springs and frame made up and put together as soon as possible, for it is at this stage when the enthusiasm gets its first real boost, particularly when the wheels are added to the chassis, for this is when you can then see the car taking shape. Up to this time there is only a pile of odd parts.

This was soon done in the case of the Ferrari, as I made use of a flat aluminium plate on which to mount the axles, very little suspension being called for on the model as none of it was visible.

The next stage was the body pattern, and from this the body parts proper, which were very soon fitted together to form a body shell. With the body shell fitted to the plate

The start of pattern making for the 1963 250 GTO Ferrari. The finished patterns together with the almost complete miniature, and the model windmill that made it possible.

27

chassis and all the wheels in place I had what looked to the eye an almost complete Ferrari model. However, I still had the engine compartment to fill, as well as all the seats, dash and controls etc. These had to be made and fitted into place, which was several months' work. Before getting half-way through this fitting out process, my enthusiasm had gone completely. I think the reason was that all these parts were being made up away from the shell and then dropped inside when complete, so that each evening I could not see, without searching, any significant improvement. In other words the model did not appear to grow in relation to the amount of hours being worked.

After about eight weeks I was very restless and often found myself absorbed in gardening rather than modelling.

Fortunately, I had a phone call from a client in London who wanted a model made of a windmill. I accepted, went straight up to town to collect the data from him, and had started on the plans by the evening. Working twelve to fourteen hours a day for the next three weeks saw the mill complete, painted and delivered and my enthusiasm back, ready to complete the Ferrari, which I did without further trouble.

I find I must see a proportionate growth in the model relative to the number of hours' work in order to maintain my enthusiasm at white heat, and I feel that it is only possible to create something worthwhile when you can work with enthusiasm. I now keep on hand in the workshop several small but interesting jobs that I can turn to to complete, should whatever I am making start to suppress my urge to move onwards. In this way any frustrations that my work may throw up can be dealt with before they can affect its quality.

I have also succeeded in overcoming problems by forming a sort of mental chest of drawers, each drawer containing the answer to a given problem. As a new subject is presented it can immediately be mentally broken down into its component parts and filed in its appropriate drawer, with a readily available set of instructions of how it can be made. This means that with very little preparation, almost any new subject can be started with the confidence that all problems can be solved. I feel this is another most vital point in creating something worthwhile, for to be single minded, which you must be, you must be free of distractions. I have not, of course, dealt in detail with the methods I use, but I feel reference to my two earlier books – *The Techniques of Ship Modelling* and *The Complete Car Modeller* – will give the reader that sort of information if, as I hope, I have whetted the appetite for 'doing' as well as appreciating the finished work.

If there is an art or craft in all of this, then I think it must be in being able to look at something and immediately be able to mentally strip it down to workable parts. I firmly believe that the appreciation of any art is enhanced by actually attempting to emulate it, whether it be music, painting or whatever. Nothing is as complicated as it first looks.

Part Three

Of all the autominiatures that I have built, and they now represent over thirty makes, the ones that have given me the most pleasure have undoubtedly been the Duesenbergs. Fate, however, took a very decisive hand in this also, for although the big 'D' was the first car that I started to build, it was not until at least seven years later that I eventually completed one. Looking back on this I feel this is how it should have been, for it is only now that I have mastered enough techniques to really do justice to the beast.

After completing the original set of wheels, the chassis frame and a set of body patterns back in 1966/67 they were put to one side because of the amount of work that they had initiated after showing them around. It was not until about 1970/71 that I had enough spare time to contemplate further work on the project. By this time I had built quite a number of car models for the now renamed National Motor Museum at Beaulieu, as well as for several collectors, all to a scale of one to twenty, and my techniques were developing along different lines. I decided to scrap the early work and start again in the new scale.

My original idea for bodywork was to use fibreglass, in fact I had made up a set of body parts for that first project. I did look at the possibility of working the bodies in sheet metal, but decided the idea was too difficult. However, one of the first sports cars that I made for the Museum Collection, was a model of a 1924 30/98 Vauxhall, with a polished aluminium body, and I knew I could not reproduce this in fibreglass. So, as with all the other skills, I set to and taught myself how to work sheet metal into car body shapes. Finding yourself in a corner like this can teach you a lot about yourself. You either do it and move on, or you don't. If you don't you have wasted all the time and effort so far put in to getting where you are. The only answer must be to 'have-a-go', very seldom do you find things as complicated as they look at first.

Another deviation from my present path in that original project, was that the main engine parts were carved from hardwood. I only use wood now for body patterns or parts of the finished bodywork where a polished wood finish is called for.

In '71, I redrew the plans to a scale of one to twenty, incorporating all the latest data that I had collected together, for although I had not had time to do any further work on the project it was in no way dead. Over the years I had been corresponding with more and more of the ACD (Auburn-Cord-Duesenberg) Club members who supplied me with photographs, dimensions, sketches and even samples of paint and upholstery from their cars. So by '72 I had a veritable pile of Duesenberg data, although I still had not actually seen a car in the flesh. I had had a very near miss though in the early years of my research. During the course of my early correspondence I received a letter from the head of a company in California, who still manufacture and supply spares for the J and SJ Duesenbergs, even though they went out of production back in 1936. My contact gave me the address of someone in Sunningdale who had several years previously ordered some spare parts from him and presumably was the owner of a Duesenberg. (As it turned out, he was the last UK owner of a big 'D'.) Of course I wrote to the address in Sunningdale, in fact I wrote several times, but did not get a reply to any of my letters. Not put off by this, I decided to drive down there and locate the car. My appetite had been whetted, if there was a big 'D' in Britain I wanted to see it, and, of course, to get some photographs of it, if this was at all possible.

Therefore, at eight o'clock one morning my wife and I headed out for Sunningdale in my battered old Standard Vanguard. After an hour or two of fruitless searching for the elusive address, I pulled into a garage in the centre of the village to fill up with petrol. I asked if they had seen an American Duesenberg in the locality and learnt that they had, in fact, rebuilt the car for the owner and had fitted the spare parts from California.

They told me the car was a 1929 model 'J', with a town car body by Barker of London. It was one of the 1929 Motor Show cars, and was in perfect condition. I could not wait to see it. Unfortunately, the owner had moved from Sunningdale to a little village called Wisborough Green, which he thought was out near Croydon, just South of London – enough said, I was on my way. The only map I had with me was in my AA

Handbook and this did not show or list the village, but I thought there was a good chance of getting some directions once I got to Croydon. However, it appeared that Wisborough Green was not very well known and no one knew where it was. We parked the car, and had some lunch. On returning to the car I noticed a taxi rank in a corner of the car park. Thinking that this was the most likely answer, as they would be bound to know the district, I went over to a group of taxi drivers and enquired, but again all I got was blank faces. Then one of them remembered something and disappeared into his cab for a pile of maps. Wisborough Green was nowhere near Croydon. It was nearly sixty miles to the south, almost down to the south coast. We got back on the road, heading south through the beautiful Sussex countryside. Wisborough Green turned out to be a typical old-style English country village, with a large village green in the centre and a scattering of cottages, a pub, church and the inevitable post office-cum-general store. As it was nearly four o'clock in the afternoon and I did not want to spend further time searching for the address, I headed for the post office to ask directions. I mentioned the name and address I was looking for and to my amazement, behind me was the person I was looking for – who said miracles do not happen?

I explained my interest and learnt to my dismay that the car was sold about twelve months before and it was now back in the USA. So, there were no Duesenbergs in Britain at all. However, he seemed very pleased to meet someone with an interest in his former masterpiece. (I have yet to meet an owner of one of these cars who looks on it as just a form of transport), and he took us back to his home and told us the story of his love for the car and his regret at having sold it. So, after a whole day, I still had not seen a big 'D' in the flesh, but I had met my first owner, a most friendly and generous person. Two qualities that fit every owner of a big 'D' that I have so far come into contact with. I also came away with a further bundle of photographs that were loaned to me for copying, to add to my files.

Returning to models, having decided to scrap my first efforts, I managed to swap them for a collection of big 'D'

photographs with a new-found ACD Club friend in Indiana, USA. I set to work and produced a set of wire wheels in the scale of one to twenty so that they would match the cars I was building for the Museum, an identical set of which I made for myself as a personal collection. I also modified the first set of tyres, in that I devised a way of reproducing the white wall tyres, so popular in the twenties and thirties, in a black and white rubber. However, this particular project was still only a hobby and commissions again overtook it and it was put to one side, as before.

Shortly after this I was asked to build the 250 GTO Ferrari, mentioned earlier, but something larger than the one to twenty scale was called for. As I have already said, I picked on one to fifteen because I think the size of model twelve to fifteen inches is just about ideal for a car model. Another point in its favour is that if a wire wheel is made to a much larger scale, it would need to have the spokes fitted singly with threaded nuts at the top of each to look correct and to me this would add unnecessary expense to an already expensive model, without adding anything to the overall character of the finished miniature.

Having completed the 1963 Ferrari, I followed it with a 1964 version and several Model 'T' Fords all to the larger scale, fitted with engine detail, opening doors and hood etc., and was very pleased with the results.

I was now getting enquiries from American collectors and in 1973 I had sufficient orders and spare models to make a trip to the States a worthwhile proposition. I considered the risk of damage or loss by air-freighting the models to overseas customers too great and thought it a much better idea to personally deliver them as this would allow me to meet my new clients and see, photograph and collect the necessary data from their cars for the models. It was also a marvellous excuse to see a real live Duesenberg.

One of the many pen-friends I had made since joining the ACD Club was a real 'enthusiast' in every sense of the word and a person with a most friendly personality, known everywhere as Doc. I had been exchanging letters with him from the start of my interest in the big 'D' and it soon became

Doc and Rosa demonstrating the folding-top mechanism for my model of the fabulous Nebraska Duesenberg, the sun really did shine on that day.

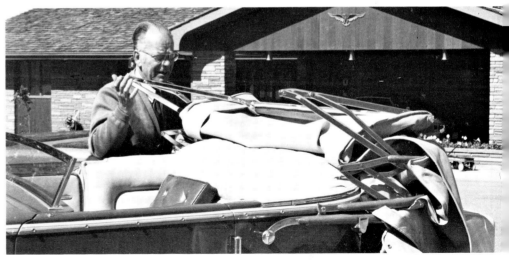

apparent that his enthusiasm for his own Duesenberg was only matched by the car's absolute beauty and perfection of design. It is a 1933 Model 'J', with outside exhaust system and a Derham Tourster body, painted in a sort of dull mid-green colour, with the chassis and underside of the fenders painted in a much lighter shade of green. However, dull the car is certainly not, for the combination of design and colouring is breathtaking and, in fact, it is recognized today as one of the most beautiful Duesenbergs ever built, and that is quite some accolade.

I then decided that this third scale of one to fifteen was that best-suited to the proposed big 'D' models. I had collected together details of almost every nut and bolt on the car and I wanted to include every one on the models. The project had also aroused a considerable amount of interest among several of my American friends and it was not long before I received a firm order for a Duesenberg model. I felt that as I had made my plans to visit the States, it would be pointless to go any further with the project before having a chance of seeing one for real.

In September 1973, my wife and I flew to Los Angeles with a small collection of models and delivered them to an enthusiastic collector. It was my first experience of American hospitality and, like their cars, it took my breath away. They must be some of the most generous and sociable people in the world. Our feet never touched the ground and we were treated like royalty.

It was at Briggs Cunningham Museum south of Los Angeles that I saw my first big 'D', a 1929 sweep panel Dual Cowl Phaeton and I was greatly impressed with this example, as I was with the other cars in that admirable collection. From LA we moved to Reno in Nevada to see the Harrah's Collection – the largest in the world – twelve hundred cars, nine of which were J and SJ Duesenbergs. I was by this time way up in the clouds, I could not work my camera fast enough, in fact we stayed in Reno an extra day so that I could get all the measurements and photographs that I needed.

From Reno we flew to Denver and spent a glorious day driving through the Rocky Mountains. By this time my wife

was beginning to dread the thought of seeing another car of whatever make. However, a cloudless day in the mountains, with the autumn colours in the trees and the first snows on the peaks, is something to banish the blues from anyone. So we were both well set for our next stage in that first US trip. This was to meet – for the first time – my, by this time, 'old friend' Doc, and to see his dream car.

We flew into Lincoln Nebraska late in the afternoon, and picked up a hire car. The next day, at about ten-thirty, we drove down to Doc's beautiful home and all my dreams came true. He took me down into his basement garage and there among several choice classics of the twenties and thirties, was the car that I had dreamt about. The one car in all the world that I longed to produce in miniature more than anything else. One can imagine my feelings when Doc offered to take it and us out for a drive on the highway.

Look at the expression on the owner's face when he looks at his classic or thoroughbred car and you will soon see whether or not he looks on it as an investment (as a lot of the newer ones do), or as a member of the family, as the true enthusiast does. As I have seen so many times, his face lit up when he proudly showed me around his 'beauty' and even more so when he got behind the steering wheel and took us all out onto the road. If the drive out was not exhilarating enough, the ride back certainly was, for I was persuaded to drive the car back myself, an ambition fulfilled if ever there was one.

By the time we left Nebraska for home I had all the measurements and photographs necessary to produce my *pièce de résistance* and another order for a model to be built.

Back in the workshop I proceeded to start a third set of Duesenberg drawings, this time to a scale of one to fifteen. I now had so much data that I had to draft two separate sheets, one for the engine and chassis and another for the bodywork. However, the project was now no longer a hobby undertaken for an odd hour or two, here and there. Now I could devote all my time to it, as it was now a full-time commission.

As all but one of the techniques had by now been perfected, it was only a matter of time before first the wheels,

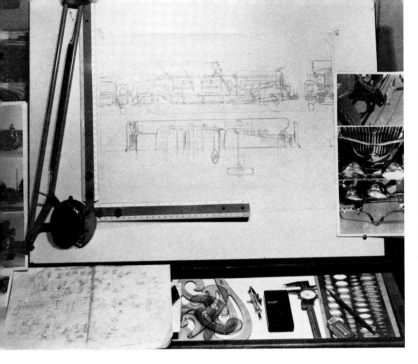

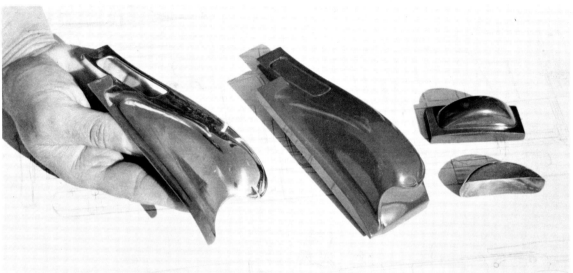

Stage two of a Wingrove miniature, to interpret into a fully detailed scale working drawing, all the data collected from the actual car. The fully detailed Duesenberg chassis before painting and one of the pure nickel fenders with its pattern and separate spare wheel-well. The complete set of electroformed fender and body parts assembled on the big 'D' chassis.

then the axles, springs, chassis frame and engine took shape. The technique I had not tried before was a method of producing the fenders and bodywork. This I had had in the back of my mind for several months after reading an article in an electronics magazine. Always on the look out for new ideas, this one involved the development of a silver paint that would conduct electricity. This, together with my knowledge of pattern making, the moulding of fibreglass, and the workings of electrolysis, led me to believe that it would be quite a simple process to reproduce almost any shape in sheet metal that I could carve in wood, by a process known as electroforming.

With the chassis complete I put my ideas into practice and with the assistance of an excellent little firm of electroplaters in Windsor, who do all my chrome and gold plating, we produced all the body and fender parts in pure nickel. With these assembled and painted I was ready by the following September, to return to the United States and personally deliver the result of my labours. It gave me great pleasure to see in the face of my clients the same look as in the face of the owner of the full-size car and this is really the reason I get so much enjoyment from my work. I do get paid for my models, one has to eat, but no amount of money in the world can switch my enthusiasm on, if the subject leaves me cold.

Another subject that really stirred my passions, was the tulipwood Hispano-Suiza. Back in early 1972 I had a phone call from a friend and client who had just taken delivery of this particular car, built originally for André Dubonnet in 1924. I was asked if I would like to build a model of it for him. Having known of the car for many years, it being one of a dozen or so that I have almost equal desires on to that of the big 'D', I just grabbed my camera and notebook, jumped in my car and was half-way to his place before he could put the phone down!

On seeing it in the flesh for the first time, it rather stunned me. The sheer size of it – almost twenty feet long – and all those pins, what had I let myself in for. Standing there with the owner, we surveyed the beauty and discussed what sort of a model she would make. I suggested that the polished woodwork might look better on the miniature if it did not have all those brass pins in it, but my client would not hear of

it. All the rivets must be included he declared. As the customer always gets what he wants, we settled on a miniature in every detail. I was a little worried though, for I could see that if the rivets were not almost as fine as a hair, on a fifteen-inch long model, then the finished work would be more akin to that of an old studded oak door.

On arriving back at my workshop I made up a small sample of bodywork, planked it and pinned it, and stained and polished it to match the colour samples I had brought back with me. I then set to in my small darkroom to develop and print up all the photographs I had brought back with me. These I enlarge up to half-plate size and mount on thick card three at a time one above the other. This not only saves having my very small workshop littered with innumerable prints, but it also allows me to always have prints, of a particular item, taken from different angles, together at all times.

With the prints and rough sketches spread out on my bench all was ready for drafting the working drawings, the scale being one to fifteen. This is always a most interesting time, for one feels that after the first few lines have started to take shape, it is almost possible to get 'under the skin' of the original designer. On a three- or four-feet-long curved outline, such as the rear deck of the Hispano or one of the pontoon fenders, I would have noted perhaps three or four dimensions relative to the ground, wheel centre or perhaps the door post. With these plotted on a blank sheet of paper, they could be joined up in any number of ways to give almost any curve. However, once the mind can be tuned into the subject that elusive shaping appears as if by magic. I also feel that to draft the plans myself in some way seems to load my fingers with all the necessary data, as to shape and proportion, to be able to build the miniature. For it is a fact that once the actual building starts, a much bigger proportion of the model is built by eye, than with continual reference and checking with the drawings. These I only use to get some initial shaping or measurement, the final shaping is always determined by my eye and my subconscious feelings for that particular part, at that moment. For this to work effectively, one needs to work alone and in a completely relaxed state of

The 1924 Hispano-Suiza nickel silver and fibreglass body parts ready for planking. The act of fitting the pearwood planks and marking out and drilling the thirteen thousand pin holes. Elaine, my able assistant, smiling at the start of the pinning operation.

mind. To assist me in this, and working as I do as a one man business in these troubled times, I need some sort of assistance most of the time, so I have fitted the workshop with a stereo cassette player. Thus, with a project such as the Hispano in front of me, and the air filled with Chopin, Schubert, Schumann or Beethoven to blot out the thoughts of the tax-man, I can enter another world.

Back to the model. With the completed drawings in one hand and the sample of bodywork in the other I returned to my client and his masterpiece for his comments. Happily these were most favourable on all counts, so I was now ready to start with the knowledge that it was possible to capture the character and finish of this magnificent beast – pinning and all. The size of the pin or rivet that I eventually used on the model was just .012 inches in diameter and I estimated that there were more than thirteen thousand of them covering the body and fenders.

The wheels and chassis frame went together in the normal way with all the usual jigs and patterns having first to be made. For the body shell I went right back to my original ideas for the first Duesenberg body, I moulded it in fibreglass. The reason being that when making the small sample of bodywork, I found it much simpler to fit the pins into blind holes about .040 inches deep than to fit them into something that had a hole right through. As it would have been almost impossible to work the necessary shapes for both body and fenders from this thickness of metal, fibreglass was the logical answer. As it was I needed to use metal, in this case a .012 inch to .020 inch-thick nickel silver sheet, for such parts as the opening hood and doors and these gave me endless problems when it came to drill all the holes, quite apart from getting the pins into place. In all, I built six models of this car, which meant marking out and drilling nearly eighty thousand .012 inch diameter holes which resulted in fifteen broken drills and much resharpening, as they became damaged or broken when working through the metal parts. I dread to think of the problems I would have had had I not used fibreglass, particularly as the tiny drills cost almost a pound each (£1).

With the fibreglass shells made, mated to the chassis and fitted out with the metal hood, doors, door frames and inside lining pieces, all was ready for the woodwork to go on. As with leather upholstery, so with wood, one should never try making use of the original materials on a miniature. A material with a scale texture of one to one looks ridiculous on a miniature with a scale of one to fifteen, even if you can then say that it is made from the same materials as the original. So this miniature tulipwood car was planked in pearwood and stained to match the original. This material has always answered all my woodworking problems, for it is as dense as plastic, with a texture and grain that can reproduce almost any other wood in miniature.

The model was covered plank for plank as per the original, with the ends tapered to accommodate the endless curves of the individual pieces. Each started life with a thickness of about .025 inches, but finished – after sanding and polishing was completed – at between .010 inches and .015 inches thick. With all the parts now planked, sanded, marked out and drilled, I must confess I was beginning to see spots before my eyes and for the first time I needed some assistance. So, after a lot of bribery and arm-twisting (they had seen me drill the holes) I persuaded my wife and two children – Mark just sixteen and Elaine thirteen – to fit most of the forty thousand .012 inch diameter pins in place for me on the first set of three cars.

Elaine achieved the greatest success placing over twenty thousand pins and it has been interesting to see just how the exercise has left its mark on her. She has since taken to moulding rubber tyres and even spoking some of the wire wheels, but I do find great difficulty in trying to encourage and develop my children's interest to my sort of work. It is not that they find any of the techniques at all complex, they are both very talented with their hands and have very active minds to go with them, but I expect I have found, as many other craftsmen-cum-familymen have, that when you live with something such as this all your life, it begins to look so easy until you actually have a go yourself. If the first attempt after a long and painful struggle does not then equal the work of the master, which it never can, then disillusion sets in and you tend to look elsewhere for your interests.

In appreciation of their assistance with the pinning of the three Hispano-Suiza models, one of their names – Mark, Elaine or Rosa – is also engraved on the underside of each of the cars alongside my own signature, which has completed every model I have built.

The only car miniature to date that I have built and not first seen in the flesh and collected the necessary data from, is the 1911 Russo Baltique. The reason being that this particular car, the winner of the 1912 Rally de Monte Carlo, is no longer in existence. The miniature was commissioned by the outstanding American periodical *Automobile Quarterly* for use in illustrating an article on this memorable St. Petersburg to Monte Carlo trip.

My clients in the United States had secured a surprising number of original photographs of the car, all taken either just before, or during the 1912 Rally. There were, however, some vital shots missing so far as I was concerned, in particular, photographs of the engine, fire wall and inside of the driver's compartment, controls etc. I did, however, get a copy of a general arrangement chassis drawing which showed one side view and one top view of the engine as well as where everything else was placed in relation to the frame. There was still one thing missing though, the plans did not contain a single dimension or scale, so although I knew where most of the detail went, I did not know how big or small to make it and evidently no-one could even locate a reference as to the size of wheel base or track of the original which I could have used as a key for the chassis drawing.

The Russian Embassy had been contacted in the USA, but they either could not or would not bother to check their files to see if they could assist with the missing data. It should perhaps be remembered that the 1912 Monte Carlo was before the Revolution. However, we had a Socialist government that was on much friendlier terms with the USSR, so I rang the Russian Trade Delegation in London to see if I could have better luck, for I had a feeling that there must be some information on this particular car, or one similar. After all, it was one of the first Russian Automobiles.

I was asked to write to them stating exactly what information I required. Within a fortnight I had made contact with a most helpful assistant at the Polytechnical Museum in Moscow, from whom I not only obtained the missing dimensions for the chassis drawing, but also plans showing the other side, and a cross section through the engine, together with sectional drawings of the gear box and back axle, including full translation from the Russian for the text on each. But what was even more exciting was that I learnt the Moscow Museum had in its display an original Russo Baltique car, although it was fitted with a different body style and of a slightly later vintage – about 1914/15.

Years ago, when collecting data to build models of Clippers and great ocean carriers of the last days of sail, that had missing or unobtainable detail, the best one could do was to copy it from others, built or owned by the same company, at around the same time, as the one being researched. So with the Russo, I asked for and got detailed photos from the 1914 car to fill in all the missing information on the 1911 model. Apart from the body and a later type of engine, the details of chassis that were comparable with the 1911 drawings were almost identical.

With the aid of the combined material from the USA and the USSR I produced a set of drawings and sent a copy to Moscow and another to New York for comment. I viewed, with some satisfaction, the corrections that both had received when they were returned – two Russian characters from the lettering on the spare wheel cover had been inadvertently drawn back to front! With this corrected and all parties happy, the model was built and used to illustrate the article on the car in *Automobile Quarterly*, *Volume 14 Number 2* and subsequently two further miniatures were also produced from the same material.

As a one man band, one not only has to look at today's work, but also to keep an eye on the road ahead, thus ensuring that the problems are minimal and the prospects worthwhile. It is so easy with creative work to spend a great deal of time with your head in the clouds, in a world of contentment and ecstasy. However, it is necessary to remember that this state is only in the mind of the thinker and that it is in the world as a whole that he lives and has to make his way. So what is the road ahead if one is to maintain an enthusiasm for one's work. This has caused me to ponder many times. I think first you must locate in yourself what motivates you and what feeds this power within.

I learnt a lesson many years ago, long before I started building car miniatures, that has stayed with me to this day. I once had an obsession with marquetry – inlayed veneer pictures. I made up dozens of kits then started designing my own, even selecting my own woods, until one day I went out with my camera and took a photograph of the main street of a particularly quaint old local village. This, through various processes, I turned into a large plan for a veneered picture. I then selected the woods and completed it to my absolute satisfaction.

To me (though I hasten to say not necessarily to everyone else) I had made a perfect job. The end result of this is that I have never been able, since, to find the necessary will-power to make another marquetry picture, even though I have tried several times. It has, since that experience, always been in the back of my mind that should I ever build a perfect car model (perfect in my eyes that is) then I could kill overnight that all important feeling that is essential for me to continue this work. It is an exceedingly fine balance that I now have to maintain between producing the best I am able, yet still leaving room for improvement. What is more, the balance will get even finer as time goes on and as my skills and techniques improve year by year, the possibility of producing in miniature a car that is 100 per cent correct in every detail, gets ever closer. However, as a businessman I am able to put against this the fact that I cannot afford the hours necessary to produce such a masterpiece and as a last resort I would have the option of refusing a commission should anyone have enough money to put forward the proposition.

The other thought that has exercised my mind recently is where do I go from here, is there a chance, after making over one hundred car models that I could get into the same sort of mental rut that I was getting into while on the factory floor.

What cleared that from my mind was an aiming point to work towards, to be my own boss and to leave my mark. What do I do when I have reached that goal? I think there are two options either to say that's enough, drop everything and start again at the bottom with a completely new venture. This has been done with success by a few, but I think only by those who have made so much money by their first efforts that should they slip out of the frying-pan on their second calling, they do not actually need to fear falling into the fire!

The second option is to direct oneself from getting to the top of a profession and maintain a position there. Though this sounds easy it can be as challenging as the first.

If you are a company chairman, you can organize people and events to eliminate your opposition, for a time at least, to maintain your position. With only yourself to deal with, the problem is much more difficult, for dealing only in stark facts as one has to, and spending all one's time reproducing objects, of any sort, one has to direct the inner self.

My aim is to slow down and consolidate my work, to improve and bring up to date my tools and techniques and above all to pick with care the commissions I undertake. Each must stir my subconscious to a feeling that 'I must make it' before I will now take on a project. Which is in truth as it should be, for a client at the end of the day is called on to part with a substantial sum of money, and he should only be asked to do this if the artist or craftsman has put something of himself into his work. When I build a model it is not an exact replica of the original (if it is it is by accident) it is my interpretation of how I see the subject. This is why I make a point of going to see, hear, touch, smell etc., each subject that I undertake to reproduce in miniature.

As I have now become so selective, are there going to be enough subjects to keep me occupied for the next twenty to thirty years, and in particular, enough cars of distinction?

Of subjects, there are plenty to keep me working for the next five hundred years, for I find the world a wonderful place. Man may be a nuisance from time to time, but at least he invented the Duesenberg!

solid silver

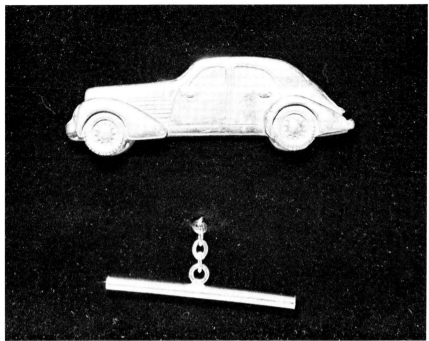

Back to jewellery, and small-scale casting patterns. Some examples of my latest intermissions between car projects. Duesenberg, Cord and Bentley miniatures as solid silver tie tacks and cufflinks, one-thirty-second scale 250 GTO Ferrari in silver plate, and a copy of the original 1936 810 Cord 'Bronze' mounted on a black marble base.

41

Of individual car subjects, I think there are just about enough to keep me going, though my aim is still to intermix them with ships, aircraft and scenic subjects as much as possible in order to make each new one seem fresh.

Of ambitions as far as projects go for the future, there are possibly three that immediately come to mind. I would like to build another large historic scenic model on the lines of Bucklers Hard. In fact I would like one big commission of this sort about every five years. I would also like to build a collection of cars in the 1/15 scale depicting the finest coachwork of the 1920s and 1930s. And lastly (a desire I have held for many, many years, that is just about to come into fruition), I would like to produce from my patterns, a collectors series of classic cars at a price that a wider range of the public can afford.

This is another of those examples where fate would seem to be turning up the right cards at just the right time. For all the parts of this jigsaw could not have come together at a more appropriate time in my career.

Way back in the Mettoy days, just after I had noticed the beautiful works that the car makers of the 1920s and 1930s had produced and before the interest and following had reached anything like the proportions of today, I tried to talk the directors into producing a collection of classics to show some of this work to the general public, but without success. Unbeknown to me, at the time, however, several other manufacturers had had similar ideas and have had some success with them.

For me at any rate, the idea had to be put into cold storage, together with another that I tried to get a publisher interested in about the same time. This was to have copies made of the ever-increasing number of my car plans which after each model has been completed are just waste paper. My original idea was to have all the drawings reproduced on the same scale, with one view of the particular car in colour, and to have printed with these a sheet containing a dozen or so of the most useful photographs. However, as a result of the success of my first motor book, *The Complete Car Modeller*, the idea has been revived and I am in the course of preparing a model car plans book.

A further development of this idea came about one day some five years ago when walking through the local market one Saturday. I noticed a stall exhibiting a large collection of very fine copper etchings. On enquiring further I found they were the work of a local man who offered to produce an etching from one of my plans. This I proceeded to let him undertake after I had added a bit of detail and shading here and there. The end result of this exercise was very pleasing indeed, and he turned out several dozen for me before stopping his spare-time enterprise for reasons beyond his control.

I visited the United States in '75 and my mind was open to ideas that could be pushed along one of those lines. Two came my way without any prompting, and were developed on my return from this trip. One was for a range of silver jewellery with car profiles as the theme, and the second was a reproduction of an original bronze model of an 810 Cord from about 1936.

Of the bronze and silver projects the former is now well on its way, and Charles T. Marshall of the Heritage Collection in California, on seeing the finished 1/32 scale bronze 810 Cord was so impressed that he commissioned a further five Classics on the same scale to form the start of a series to be called *Grand Touring Cars of the World*. Each master will have produced from it 2,500 castings numbered and signed. To go with these will be a limited edition of 2,500 of each of the original plans, to be etched or printed on stainless steel with one view shown in colour.

So another ambition though conceived many years ago is now seeing the light of day. I know not how the events and people find their way into my orbit, but I am forever grateful to whoever put them there, my only hope is that my work may keep them happy.

Chronology and model data

1911 Type 'C' 24/30 h.p. Russo Baltique

(1:15 scale)

The winner of the 1912 Monte Carlo Rally built for *Automobile Quarterly* from data supplied by Alec Ulmann and the Polytechnic Museum, Moscow. This is the only marque not to have been viewed prior to work commencing on the model.

1912
35J Mercer
Raceabout

(1:20 scale)

Data collected from the
'Harrah's Collection' car in
Reno, Nevada, USA. Originally
for a National Motor Museum
model though several others
have also been produced from
the same material. Bright work
is gold-plated to simulate
polished brass.

1912
Model 'T' Ford

(1:15 scale)

Data originally collected from a 4 seat tourer body for a model now in the Evoluon Museum in Holland. However, after completing the commission I felt the need to produce something more befitting the character of the 'tin lizzie', so I built several further examples with this runabout body.

48

1913 Prince Henry Vauxhall (1:20 scale)

The start of my commissions for the National Motor Museum Collection and the first car model to be fully scratch built from my own plans. This is also one of the few models to be built as a 'one off'.

1924 (Tulipwood) Hispano-Suiza

(1:15 scale)

This is the famed Dubonnet car with the planked body by Nieuport. The model is planked in pear wood and fitted with over 13,000 brass pins. Several miniatures have been built showing the car as it is today with the planked pontoon fenders. After some research I found that the original fender line was very different and to my mind more in keeping with the 1920s styling. The swept aluminium wings show the car as it was in 1924/25.

1925 12/50 (Ducks Back) Alvis

(1:20 scale)

Another interesting example of the 1920s vogue, with a polished aluminium body.

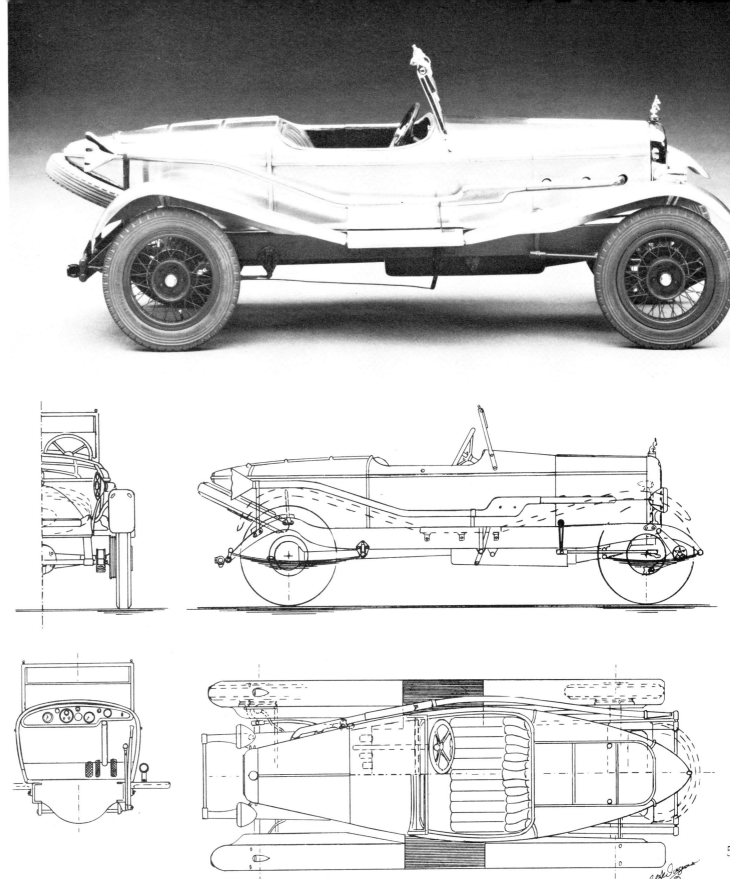

1927
Black Hawk
Stutz Speedster

(1:20 scale)

Another of the outstanding cars from the 'Harrah Collection' in Reno, USA used as a subject for a miniature for the National Motor Museum Collection.

1927
Type 43 Bugatti

(1:20 scale)

A most interesting example
from this family of classics,
particularly from the modeller's
point of view, with regard to
the unique wheel construction.

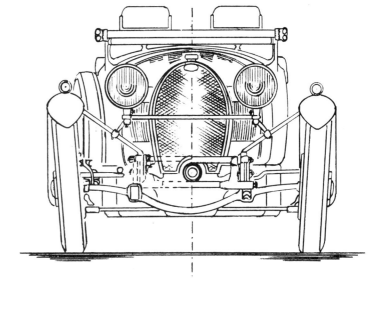

1928
Black Hawk
Stutz Speedster

(1:20 scale)

Built basically from the same
plans as the 1927 car, but with
slight detail changes and a most
attractive colour scheme
authenticated after further
research.

64

1929
4½ Litre (Blower) Bentley

(1:15 scale)

This Bentley must be *the* English sports car and of all the Bentleys the one that stirs the blood the most, which is rather strange for it was an unsuccessful design, which never actually won a race. The subject of the model is one of the Paget-Birkin team cars. Five models have been built, four painted dark green etc., to match the original and one, for my own collection, has been left unpainted to show the detailing and work involved more clearly. A most exciting project to complete.

1930 1750
Alfa Romeo

(1:20 scale)

One of a trio, and the third of
the set. The subject of the
model was in fact black as were
the first two models. I felt a
more befitting colour for the
Alfa was red, hence this
example.

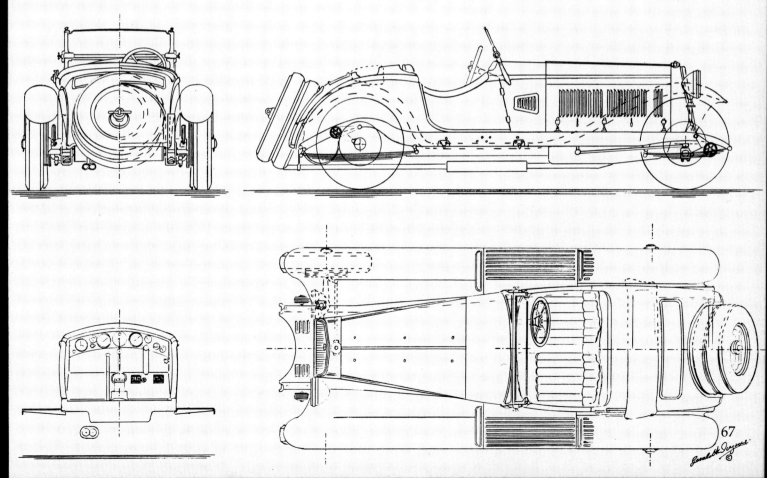

67

1930
Lea-Francis
Hyper Sports

(1:20 scale)

Not one of my favourite
models, though it made a name
for itself in its day on the track,
so earning a place in the
National Motor Museum
Collection. The fabric body is
simulated with the aid of
cellulose paint on an aluminium
shell.

LV 8301

1930 Brooklands Riley

(1:20)

Evidently a very popular car with the racing enthusiast who likes to maximize his performance. Most full-size examples have been much modified as was the subject for this model. Considerable research was necessary to show in the miniature the car as it left the factory.

1930
4½ Litre
'S' Type Invicta

(1:20 scale)

An extremely attractive piece of machinery and one that gave me much pleasure building. For me, like the Alfa Romeo, a car that looks as though it is going somewhere even when standing at the kerb.

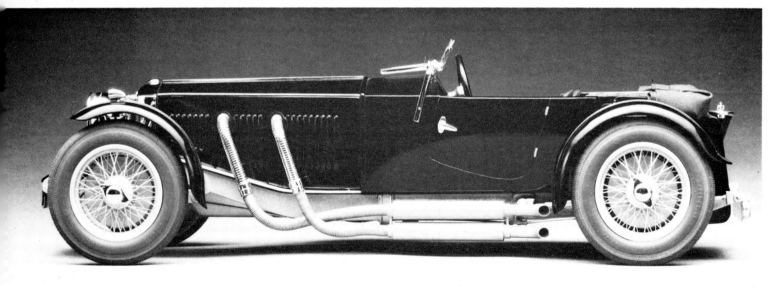

1931 Model 'J' Duesenberg

(1:15 scale)

To me the subject is perfection and gave me many months of pleasure while creating this 15 inch long miniature. Though several examples of this body style have been produced, only one has been given this colour scheme. The full size original masterpiece is housed in California, USA.

1932 'TT'Replica Frazer Nash

(1:20 scale)

There is always a fascination for me when I see my subject for the first time. Some cars are totally uninspiring and leave me cold, while others are exciting on sight even before learning anything about them. This model fell well and truly into the latter category.

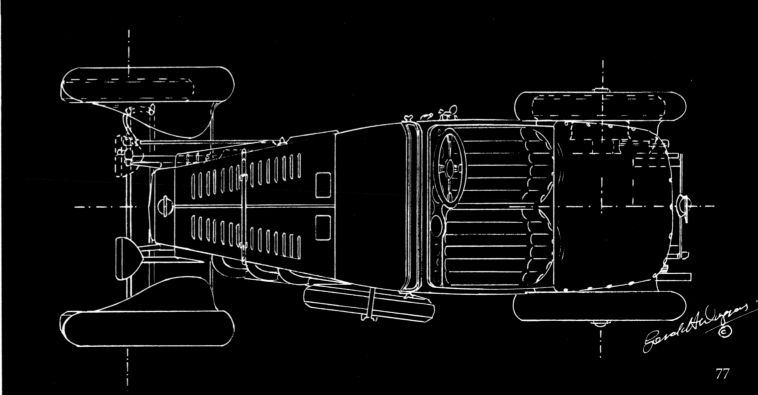

1933 'SJ' Duesenberg with Weymann Speedster Body

(1:15 scale)

Another ambition fulfilled. When I learnt of the fabulous Harrah Automobile Collection in Reno, Nevada, I learnt also of this car's existence. Though anything but practical, being 20 feet long, almost a two seater (only some 38 inches across the front seat), and capable of over 100 m.p.h. in second gear, its design is nonetheless perfection and one of my favourites.

1933 'J' Duesenberg with Derham Tourster Body

(1:15 scale)

For me this is the most beautiful piece of machinery man ever put on four wheels and represents a long-standing ambition that was amply fulfilled when I first saw it in the flesh, drove it and modelled it. Like the Weymann Speedster Duesenberg, a design from the hand of Gordon M. Buehrig, the world's greatest designer of the all time classics.

1933 MG (J2) Midget

(1:20 scale)

The original J.2. commission for the National Motor Museum. All black with red seats and wheels. With the data collected for this miniature was a list of the two-tone colour schemes available for the swept fender style which I felt looked more interesting. However, two models were built with cycle fenders, the second having white wheels, red seats and black body.

1934 MG (J2) Midget

(1:20 scale)

The first of the swept fender cars. The second one was painted in two-tone green and now lives in California, USA. Other colours available were two-tone blue, two-tone grey and ivory and fawn. Incidentally the ex-works price was £199.10s (£199.50).

1934 M45 Lagonda

(1:20 scale)

Winner of the 1935 Le Mans race averaging over 77 m.p.h. for the 24 hours. A commission for the National Motor Museum Collection. Three miniatures were built showing the car at the time of the race.

1935
Aston Martin
Ulster

(1:20 scale)

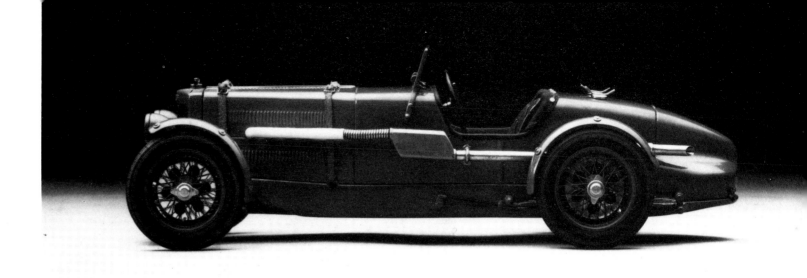

Another car like the Brooklands Riley, much favoured by the racing enthusiast and it would seem inevitably much modified. As the commissions for the National Motor Museum require to show the car 'as it left the factory' quite a lot of research is needed in some instances to correct the data collected for these models.

1963 250 GTO Ferrari

(1:15 scale)

The original of three models built from data collected from this car. The other two do not have the white lines over the roof. This is the first of my models to be built in the 1:15 scale, and the first to have engine detail, opening doors and working door-catches.

88

1964 250 GTO Ferrari

(1:15 scale)

Built at the same time as the 1963 cars, with the bodies produced by a new technique whereby each was formed in a mould by spraying molten metal to a thickness of about one-sixteenth of an inch. The model is complete with engine detail, opening doors and hood.

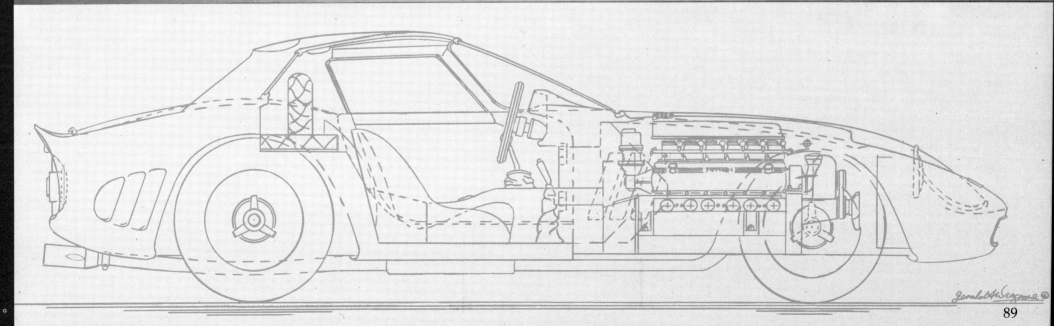

1967 BT24
Repco Brabham

(1:20 scale)

The second car model to be completely scratch built from my own plans and the first of the world championship collection of Grand Prix cars for the National Motor Museum.

1968
Gold Leaf
Team Lotus

(1:20 scale)

The first of my Ford Cosworth powered winners. Like many others, I was to become very familiar with this engine. A most pleasing and compact piece of machinery to model. The G.P. cars are the only ones I have built in this scale to contain engine detail.

1969
Matra Ford

(1:20 scale)

Jackie Stewart's winning car. It was while building this model that I received a telephone call from another artist craftsman to enquire whether or not I could make use of his services, which were, would you believe, in the field of lettering and the preparation of artwork for the silk-screen printer. Bryan Beddows has since this time produced all the artwork for my G.P. models.

1971
Tyrrell Ford

(1:20 scale)

Another of Jackie Stewart's winning cars. Not to my mind a pretty car, but from the practical point of view a most successful one. Artwork by Bryan Beddows.

1972
JPS Lotus
(1:20 scale)

The Grand Prix cars are not among my favourite subjects. This car, however, is an exception with a design that is a complete concept rather than a place for wrapping up the driver, engine and suspension in any convenient shape and putting stickers all over it. Artwork by Bryan Beddows.

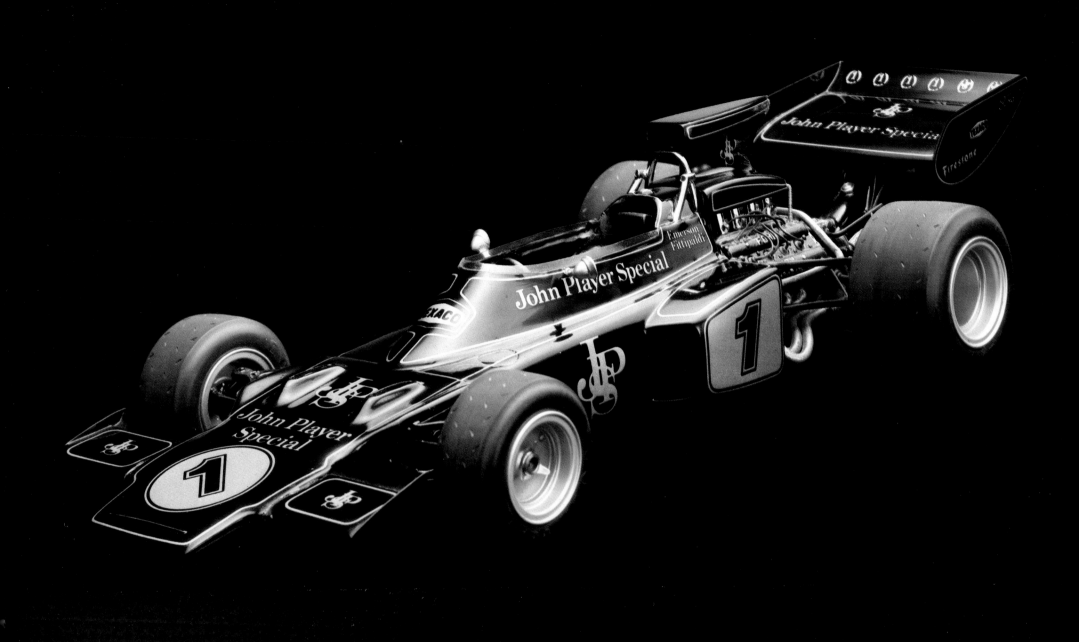
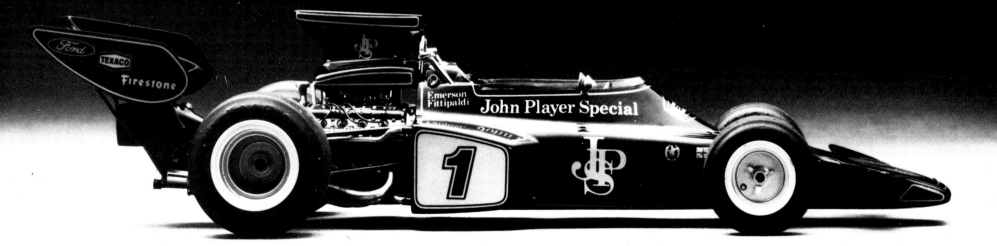

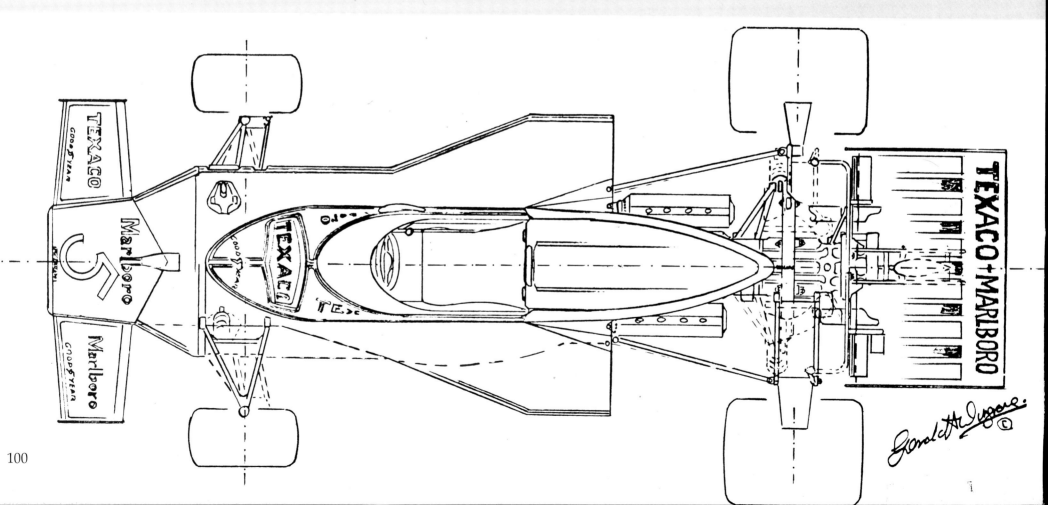

100

1974
M23 McLaren

(1:20 scale)

Note the influence of the advertising man and compare it with the days of the Repco, was I pleased to have had that unexpected phone-call back in '69. Lettering is not one of my strong points – we all have our limitations! Artwork by Bryan Beddows.

1975
312 Ferrari

(1:20 scale)

Niki Lauda's winning car.
Photographed and measured up
on the practice day for the
British Grand Prix. As is the
practice with all my work either
the owner or manufacturer (in
this case Ferrari in Italy), check
out the plans before work
commences on the miniature.
Artwork by Bryan Beddows.

Grand Touring Cars of the world

The start of a limited edition series for the discerning collector, to be produced in gold, silver and pewter with the original working drawings produced as framed stainless steel etchings.

The following six miniatures are the original patterns, fabricated from brass, nickel silver, and bronze, for a collectors series. Each will have produced from it just 2,500 numbered copies. The first few will be in solid silver and/or gold, with the remainder in pewter. Each will hold the Artist's signature and all are to the same scale of 1:32, making each miniature about six inches long.

1909 40/50 h.p.
Rolls Royce
(1:32 scale)

1931 Murphy Duesenberg

(1:32 scale)

1936 810 Cord

(1:32 scale)

1927 Type 43 Bugatti

(1:32 scale)

1935 SSK
Mercedes Benz
(1:32 scale)

1963 250
GTO Ferrari
(1:32 scale)

Index